STUDY GUIDE

Copyright © 2022 by Rodney Gage

Published by Inspire

All rights reserved. No portion of this book may be reproduced, stored in a retrieval system, or transmitted in any form or by any means—electronic, mechanical, photocopy, recording, scanning, or other—except for brief quotations in critical reviews or articles, without prior written permission of the author.

Scripture quotations marked NIV are taken from the Holy Bible, New International Version®, NIV®. Copyright © 1973, 1978, 1984, 2011 by Biblica, Inc.™ Used by permission of Zondervan. All rights reserved worldwide. www.zondervan.com. The "NIV" and "New International Version" are trademarks registered in the United States Patent and Trademark Office by Biblica, Inc.™ | Scripture quotations marked NKJV are taken from the New King James Version®. Copyright © 1982 by Thomas Nelson. Used by permission. All rights reserved. | Scripture quotations marked NLT are taken from the Holy Bible, New Living Translation, copyright © 1996, 2004, 2015 by Tyndale House Foundation. Used by permission of Tyndale House Publishers, Inc., Carol Stream, Illinois 60188. All rights reserved. | Scripture quotations marked TPT are from The Passion Translation®. Copyright © 2017, 2018 by Passion & Fire Ministries, Inc. Used by permission. All rights reserved. ThePassionTranslation.com.

For foreign and subsidiary rights, contact the author.

Cover design by: Eric Powell
Cover Photo by: Andrew van Tilborgh

ISBN: 978-1-957369-15-0   1 2 3 4 5 6 7 8 9 10

Printed in the United States of America

STUDY GUIDE

THE DOUBLE WIN

8 QUESTIONS EVERYONE MUST ASK
TO WIN AT WORK AND AT HOME

RODNEY GAGE

CONTENTS

Chapter 1. A No-Win Situation 6

Chapter 2. The Motives Question:
What's Driving Your Decisions? 12

Chapter 3. The Beliefs Question:
Who or What Makes You Happy? 18

Chapter 4. The Dream Question:
What Does Your Future Look Like? 26

Chapter 5. The Values Question:
What Do You Want to Be Known For? 32

Chapter 6. The Priorities Question:
What's (Really) Important to You? 38

Chapter 7. The Expectations Question:
Who Does What by When? 46

Chapter 8. The Success Question:
How Do You Define the Win? 52

Chapter 9. The Legacy Question:
How Will You Influence the Next Generation? 58

Introduction

A NO-WIN SITUATION

Is it even possible to live a life that's healthy, functional, and fulfilling—at work and at home? The answer is "yes!"

Reading Time

As you read the Introduction: "A No-Win Situation?" in *The Double Win*, review, reflect on, and respond to the text by answering the following questions.

What dream have you pursued or situation have you endured that has pushed you and/or your family to its limits?

_____
_____
_____
_____
_____

At what moment did you come face to face with the stark reality that you were on an unsustainable trajectory, and something had to give? What did that moment look like?

_____
_____
_____
_____
_____

In your own life, or in the life of someone you know, how have you seen stress at work affect family life?

_____
_____
_____
_____
_____
_____

Reflect on

Matthew 11:28-30 (TPT):

"Are you weary, carrying a heavy burden? Come to me. I will refresh your life, for I am your oasis. Simply join your life with mine. Learn my ways and you'll discover that I'm gentle, humble, easy to please. You will find refreshment and rest in me. For all that I require of you will be pleasant and easy to bear."

Consider the scripture above and answer the following questions:

In what ways is Jesus an oasis for the burdened and weary?

_____
_____
_____
_____
_____
_____
_____

What habits might a person need to learn so they can find refreshment and rest in Him?

_____
_____
_____
_____
_____
_____
_____

How would you encourage someone who is fearful in that they consider Jesus' invitation to be just another burden that will be neither pleasant nor easy to bear?

_____
_____
_____
_____
_____
_____
_____
_____
_____
_____
_____

How have you seen stress in the family affect the person's productivity and relationships at work?

_____
_____
_____
_____
_____

Which of the statistics and descriptions of stress stand out to you? Why are these significant?

_____
_____
_____
_____
_____

In general, based on your personal "wiring," and the examples of the leaders in your life, which area—work or family—are you more likely to prioritize over the other?

_____
_____
_____
_____
_____

How do you deal with the tension between work and family and the responsibility that both require?

_____
_____
_____
_____

Rodney proposes three ways people can position themselves for the double win:

- Be honest with at least one person about where you are right now.
- Involve people in the solution to get you to a healthier place.
- Be equally hopeful and tenacious as you cut new grooves in your neural pathways.

Which do you anticipate will be the most challenging?

_____
_____
_____
_____
_____

What do you hope to get out of this book?

_____
_____
_____
_____
_____
_____
_____

chapter 1

THE MOTIVES QUESTION: WHAT'S DRIVING YOUR DECISIONS?

KEY PRINCIPLE: KNOW YOUR WHY.

The factor that drives our decisions is found in one word: more. The push to have more stuff, make more money, be more successful, and be more impressive erodes (or clobbers) any sense of margin.

Reading Time

As you read Chapter 1: "The Motives Question: What's Driving Your Decisions?" in *The Double Win*, review, reflect on, and respond to the text by answering the following questions.

If "margin" is the space between events that gives you time to breathe, think, and rest, if only for a few moments, how much margin do you have in your life? To what do you attribute that?

_____
_____
_____
_____
_____
_____
_____
_____

What are some symptoms of "hurry sickness"? Do you suffer from any of them? Explain your answer.

_____
_____
_____
_____
_____
_____
_____
_____
_____
_____
_____

Reflect on

Luke 10:40-42 (TPT):

Martha became exasperated with finishing the numerous household chores . . . so she interrupted Jesus and said, "Lord, don't you think it's unfair that my sister left me to do all the work by myself? You should tell her to get up and help me."

The Lord answered her, "Martha, my beloved Martha. Why are you upset and troubled, pulled away by all these many distractions? Mary has discovered the one thing most important by choosing to sit at my feet."

Consider the scripture above and answer the following questions:

When do you find yourself feeling like Martha?

_____
_____
_____
_____
_____
_____

When do you find yourself feeling like Mary?

_____
_____
_____
_____
_____
_____

How can you and those who share your life work together so you all have time for worship?

_____
_____
_____
_____

If you can't get them to help, which would be a healthier choice: work or worship?

_____
_____
_____
_____

Which of the following lies have you heard come out of your mouth? By believing that lie, what do you expect the payoff to be?
- "There's not enough time to do everything I have to do!"
- "I'm just in a busy season right now. It'll be different soon."
- "But this is really important!"

___

What are your limitations? How difficult is it for you to admit you have them? Explain your answer.

___

How would regularly pruning your commitments change your pace, your mindset, and your relationships? Why do people neglect pruning?

___

What are some practical, specific ways you can "bring God into the mix"? What difference will it make?

Look at your schedule, and take some time to list all of your responsibilities.
- What's truly important?

- What seems urgent but may need to be pruned?

- What's the payoff of staying so busy?

- What's the payoff of building in more margin?

chapter 2

THE BELIEFS QUESTION: WHO OR WHAT MAKES YOU HAPPY?

KEY PRINCIPLE: HAPPINESS IS A CHOICE.

We're aware of our choices and emotions, but the driving, shaping, unseen force underneath them is our belief system.

Reading Time

As you read Chapter 2: "The Beliefs Question: Who or What Makes You Happy?" in *The Double Win*, review, reflect on, and respond to the text by answering the following questions.

How, traditionally, have you thought of the human "heart"? How do the following verses support or challenge your thinking?

- "Above all else, guard your heart, for everything you do flows from it" (Proverbs 4:23, NIV).

- "For as he thinks in his heart, so is he" (Proverbs 23:7, NKJV).

- "Don't you know that when you allow even a little lie into your heart, it can permeate your entire belief system?" (Galatians 5:9, TPT).

Reflect on

2 Corinthians 10:3-5 (NIV):

For though we live in the world, we do not wage war as the world does. The weapons we fight with are not the weapons of the world. On the contrary, they have divine power to demolish strongholds. We demolish arguments and every pretension that sets itself up against the knowledge of God, and we take captive every thought to make it obedient to Christ.

Consider the scripture above and answer the following questions:

Reflect on your words, your emotions, and the consequences of your choices over the past couple of days. What deeply ingrained false beliefs about God, yourself, and the way life ought to go do they uncover?

_____
_____
_____
_____
_____

What are some practical steps you can take to wage siege warfare against your false beliefs and drive the truth about Jesus deep into your mind and heart?

_____
_____
_____
_____
_____

What difference will it make?

Think back over the course of your life—especially your childhood and pivotal events. Make a list of the most significant events.

_____
_____
_____
_____
_____
_____
_____

How did these shape your beliefs about your value, your safety, your potential, and your competence?

_____
_____
_____
_____
_____
_____
_____

Think about people in the news and maybe some you know (Write in code if that person is sitting near you!), and try to identify what they boast in.

_____
_____
_____
_____

Do you think the term "idolatry" or "counterfeit gods" is too harsh to describe misplaced priorities? Explain your answer.

_____
_____
_____
_____

What can you do to develop each of the four habits described in this chapter?
- Shift your perspective.

_____
_____
_____
_____

- Don't let others highjack your purpose.

_____
_____
_____
_____

- Worry less, and trust God more.

_____
_____
_____
_____
_____

- Stay focused on your purpose, not your problem.

_____
_____
_____
_____
_____
_____

In what ways can the following statement be true?

> *"Happiness comes from serving others—giving your life away."*

_____
_____
_____
_____
_____
_____
_____
_____

chapter 3

THE DREAM QUESTION: WHAT DOES YOUR FUTURE LOOK LIKE?

KEY PRINCIPLE: LIFE'S A JOURNEY, NOT A DESTINATION.

It's never too late. Sure, we bring our wounds and scars with us on the trip, but God can weave our heartaches into a new, beautiful fabric.

Reading Time

As you read Chapter 3: "The Dream Question: What Does Your Future Look Like?" in *The Double Win*, review, reflect on, and respond to the text by answering the following questions.

Compare and contrast the two ideas presented in this chapter regarding the ideal future:

a) I'm waiting to arrive at a heaven-on-earth stage of ease and plenty.

b) It's all about the journey, not the destination.

_____
_____
_____
_____
_____
_____
_____
_____
_____
_____
_____
_____

Which idea most closely aligns with your view?

_____
_____
_____
_____
_____

Reflect on

Habakkuk 2:2-3 (NIV):

*Write down the revelation
and make it plain on tablets
o that a herald may run with it.
For the revelation awaits an appointed time;
it speaks of the end
and will not prove false.
Though it linger, wait for it;
it will certainly come
and will not delay."*

Consider the scripture above and answer the following questions:

What revelation has God given you that you have neglected to write down? What has stopped you?

_____
_____
_____
_____
_____
_____
_____
_____
_____
_____
_____
_____
_____

How might writing it down help you while you're waiting for it to come to fruition? Consider the benefits Rodney mentions:
- It forces us to clarify what we really want.
- It motivates us to take action.
- It provides a filter to assess other opportunities.
- It helps us overcome hindrances and resistance.
- It enables us to see and celebrate progress.

_____
_____
_____
_____
_____
_____
_____
_____
_____

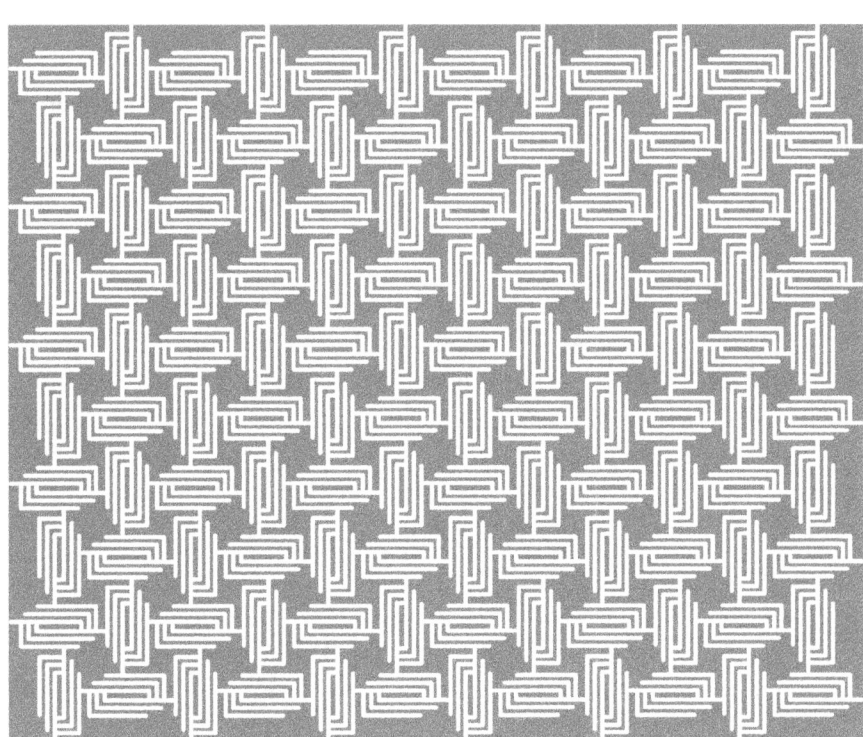

How has it shaped your personal and professional core values?

___

What gifts, talents, and other resources has God put into your hands?

___

If you were God, how would you use a person like you?

___

Why is it important to see the journey as the mission, not just the destination?

___

Which of the misguided dreams and distractions have gotten people you know off track? (If that person is sitting next to you, use hieroglyphics!)

_____
_____
_____
_____
_____

What have been the consequences in that person's life and relationships?

_____
_____
_____
_____
_____

How hard is it for you to find the balance of reaching for the stars and being rigorously realistic?

_____
_____
_____
_____
_____

Do you need a wake-up call? Why or why not?

_____
_____
_____
_____
_____

chapter 4

THE VALUES QUESTION: WHAT DO YOU WANT TO BE KNOWN FOR?

KEY PRINCIPLE: SIGNIFICANCE IS MORE IMPORTANT THAN SUCCESS.

Every day (and in fact, every minute), we have a choice to pursue success defined by power, possessions, and prestige . . . or to pursue God's purpose for us.

Reading Time

As you read Chapter 4: "The Values Question: Who Do You Want to Be Known For?" in *The Double Win*, review, reflect on, and respond to the text by answering the following questions.

What are some reasons it's so easy to slip into self-effort instead of trusting God, and self-promotion instead of humility and gratitude?

As you think about passages of scripture that have been meaningful to you, what values stand out?

Reflect on

Romans 12:1-2 (TPT):

Beloved friends, what should be our proper response to God's marvelous mercies? To surrender yourselves to God to be his sacred, living sacrifices. And live in holiness, experiencing all that delights his heart. For this becomes your genuine expression of worship.

Stop imitating the ideals and opinions of the culture around you, but be inwardly transformed by the Holy Spirit through a total reformation of how you think. This will empower you to discern God's will as you live a beautiful life, satisfying and perfect in his eyes.

Consider the scripture above and answer the following questions:

Which ideals and opinions of culture are you most tempted to embrace?

_____
_____
_____
_____
_____

What is it about those ideals that lures you?

_____
_____
_____
_____
_____
_____

How can you go about letting the Holy Spirit transform your thinking so your values are more likely to delight God's heart?

_____
_____
_____
_____
_____

If you're not sure about the previous question, or you lack the ability to let the world's values go, who can you ask to help you? What's your next step?

_____
_____
_____
_____
_____

When have you seen people (maybe even yourself) craft their values: from the beginning, in the middle of struggles, or after a calamity?

___

What are the benefits and liabilities of crafting them in each stage?

___

Why is it so important to *live* our values—not just state them—in front of our families?

___

Take time to reflect (or continue to reflect) on these questions:
- What do I want to be known for?

___

- What's important in our marriage?

___

- What beliefs and lifestyle do I want to impart to my children (and grandchildren)?

_____
_____
_____
_____

What influence do I want to have on the people around me (neighbors, friends, colleagues)?

_____
_____
_____
_____

How can I live so that God will one day say to me, *"Well done, good and faithful servant? Enter into the joy of your Master!"*

_____
_____
_____
_____

Now, what are the values you're committed to living by? Talk about them, write them, and rewrite them until they're just right. Then post them in a conspicuous place where your family can see them every day.

_____
_____
_____
_____
_____

chapter 5

THE PRIORITIES QUESTION: WHAT'S (REALLY) IMPORTANT TO YOU?

**KEY PRINCIPLE:
SAY "NO" TO THE GOOD, SO YOU CAN SAY "YES" TO THE BEST.**

Make sure your commitments reflect your priorities. When we know what's important "prior" to a decision, we can say "no" to the good, so we can say "yes" to the best.

Reading Time

As you read Chapter 5: "The Priorities Question: What's (Really) Important to You?" in *The Double Win*, review, reflect on, and respond to the text by answering the following questions.

What causes people to make New Year's Resolutions?

_____
_____
_____
_____
_____
_____
_____

If you've made New Year's Resolutions, how much have they cost? How much have they paid in return?

_____
_____
_____
_____
_____
_____
_____
_____
_____
_____
_____
_____
_____
_____
_____

Reflect on

2 Corinthians 12:8-10 (NLT):

"Three different times I begged the Lord to take it away. Each time he said, "My grace is all you need. My power works best in weakness." So now I am glad to boast about my weaknesses, so that the power of Christ can work through me. That's why I take pleasure in my weaknesses, and in the insults, hardships, persecutions, and troubles that I suffer for Christ. For when I am weak, then I am strong."

Consider the scripture above and answer the following questions:

What is your gut instinct when you think of your "thorn in the flesh"?

_____
_____
_____
_____
_____
_____

How does it keep you reliant on God?

_____
_____
_____
_____
_____
_____
_____

In what ways does your attitude mirror the apostle Paul's: "I take pleasure in my weaknesses . . . for when I am weak, then I am strong"?

_____
_____
_____
_____
_____

Ask the Holy Spirit to help you see your thorn the way He does. And, ask Him to open your eyes—physical and spiritual—to the reality of God's grace.

_____
_____
_____
_____
_____
_____

On a scale of 0 (not on the radar) to 10 (off the charts), how would you rate your current success and fulfillment in each of these areas? Explain your rating for each one.

Your faith _____

_____
_____
_____
_____

Your most important relationships _____

_____
_____
_____
_____

Your values _____

_____
_____
_____
_____

Your calling _____

_____
_____
_____
_____

Your growth _____

_____
_____
_____
_____

Take some time to plan for one step you want to take in each of these areas.

_____
_____
_____
_____
_____
_____

Now, look at the other areas. Create a workable, effective plan to "fertilize" your heart, prioritize your relationships, stretch your mind, and make you physically stronger. What do you need to say "no" to so you can say "yes" to what's most important?

_____
_____
_____
_____
_____
_____
_____
_____
_____

Which of the five "roadblocks and dead ends" have you experienced in the past few years?

- ☐ A Misplaced Why
- ☐ Distractions
- ☐ Trouble
- ☐ Opposition
- ☐ Fear

How did you respond?

_____
_____
_____
_____

Which ones are you experiencing now?

_____
_____
_____
_____

What difference does it (or will it) make to see these as tests to help you grow wiser and stronger?

_____
_____
_____
_____

chapter 6

THE EXPECTATIONS QUESTION: WHO DOES WHAT BY WHEN?

**KEY PRINCIPLE:
IT TAKES TEAMWORK
TO MAKE THE DREAM WORK.**

We're creatures of habit—we react the same way to the same things over and over again. To change and create new, healthy habits, we need to invest our hearts and minds in new responses

Reading Time

As you read Chapter 6: "The Expectations Question: Who Does What by When?" in *The Double Win*, review, reflect on, and respond to the text by answering the following questions.

How much of a team player are you? On what do you base your opinion?

_____
_____
_____
_____
_____
_____
_____
_____
_____

Think of the last interpersonal tension you experienced. What was the difference between your expectation (or someone's expectation of you) and reality?

_____
_____
_____
_____
_____
_____
_____
_____
_____
_____
_____

Reflect on

Romans 12:12-16 (NLT):

Rejoice in our confident hope. Be patient in trouble, and keep on praying. When God's people are in need, be ready to help them. Always be eager to practice hospitality.

Bless those who persecute you. Don't curse them; pray that God will bless them. Be happy with those who are happy, and weep with those who weep. Live in harmony with each other. Don't be too proud to enjoy the company of ordinary people. And don't think you know it all!

Consider the scripture above and answer the following questions:

As a creature of habit, what is your normal reaction to trouble, persecution, cursing, and weeping?

_____
_____
_____
_____
_____

Write a prayer to the Holy Spirit asking Him to inspire new responses in you and cause them to become habitual.

_____
_____
_____
_____
_____
_____

_____

_____

_____

_____

_____

_____

_____

What will it look like to invest your heart and mind in these new responses?

_____

_____

_____

_____

What are some of the painful consequences that happen when we fail to meet another person's expectations . . . and when they fail to meet ours?

_____
_____
_____
_____
_____

How do you think your childhood experiences shaped your expectations and reactions to disagreements?

_____
_____
_____
_____

Which of the relationship skills discussed in this chapter are the most challenging for you and those you love?
- Value the team.
- Develop negotiating skills.
- Practice confession and repentance.
- Become more comfortable with disagreement.

_____
_____
_____
_____
_____
_____

What specific negotiating skills do you need to develop? What difference will it (or they) make?

_____
_____
_____
_____
_____
_____
_____

What's the power of confession and repentance in a relationship? Does owning your part in a strained relationship terrify you, make you angry, or inspire you? Explain your answer.

_____
_____
_____
_____
_____
_____
_____
_____

Take some time to discuss these topics with your spouse, or if you're single, with a close friend: "What's important to us/me?" and "Who do we want to become as a family?"

_____
_____
_____
_____

chapter 7

THE SUCCESS QUESTION: HOW DO YOU DEFINE THE WIN?

**KEY PRINCIPLE:
THOSE WHO KNOW YOU BEST
LOVE YOU THE MOST.**

Marriage. Children. Career. Many of us find all kinds of excuses to avoid making necessary changes. We put them off, but time is a precious and fleeting commodity.

Reading Time

As you read Chapter 7: "The Success Question: How Do You Define the Win?" in *The Double Win*, review, reflect on, and respond to the text by answering the following questions.

Think of an area in your life that you have matured. In which stage of the Ann Landers Father's Day column are you? How is your thinking during this stage different than the earlier stages?

_____
_____
_____
_____
_____
_____
_____
_____

Which of the points about investing in your marriage—love deeply, forgive quickly, choose joy, and live intentionally—do you need to apply today? What difference will it make?

_____
_____
_____
_____
_____
_____
_____
_____

Reflect on

Psalm 39:4-5 (NLT):

*Lord, remind me how brief my time on earth will be.
Remind me that my days are numbered—
how fleeting my life is.
You have made my life no longer than the width of my hand.
My entire lifetime is just a moment to you;
at best, each of us is but a breath.*

Consider the scripture above and answer the following questions:

What tension do you feel between not having enough time to invest in what really matters but thinking you have plenty of time to do something about it?

_____
_____
_____
_____
_____

How would you live if you truly believed that your days were numbered?

_____
_____
_____
_____
_____

What aspects of that life can you implement now?

_____
_____
_____
_____
_____
_____
_____
_____
_____
_____
_____
_____

Which of the points about investing in your children—giving direction, being available, and providing loving discipline—need some attention? What are some specific adjustments you'll make?

_____
_____
_____
_____

Which of the attitude adjustments—be thankful for your job, be faithful right now, and commit to excellence—do you need to work on? Who will notice?

_____
_____
_____
_____

Why do you think it's important to identify the payoffs of bad habits and then identify better ones to encourage change?

_____
_____
_____
_____

Take some time to reflect and write your analysis of why bad habits have looked attractive to you. What better habits can take their place? What will their payoffs be, and what do you need to keep you going on this new path? You can use this template for each habit:

Bad habit: _____

_____

_____

The attractive but unhelpful payoff:_____

_____

_____

A better habit: _____

_____

_____

A more attractive payoff: _____

_____

_____

Sources of strength and tenacity: _____

_____

_____

Do you think a "double win" at home and at work is really possible for you? Explain your answer.

_____

_____

_____

_____

_____

_____

chapter 8

THE LEGACY QUESTION: HOW WILL YOU INFLUENCE THE NEXT GENERATION?

**KEY PRINCIPLE:
WHAT YOU LEAVE IN THEM
IS MORE IMPORTANT THAN
WHAT YOU LEAVE FOR THEM.**

Nothing else was more important to my father-in-law than those three things. His definition of success was "Those who know you best love you the most."

Reading Time

As you read Chapter 8: "The Legacy Question: How Will You Influence the Next Generation?" in *The Double Win*, review, reflect on, and respond to the text by answering the following questions.

When you hear the word "inheritance," what comes to mind? Along that vein, what do you hope to leave as an inheritance to your progeny?

_____
_____
_____
_____
_____
_____
_____
_____
_____

What legacy of values and character have your parents and grandparents passed down to you? How do you think that legacy has affected you and your most important relationships?

_____
_____
_____
_____
_____
_____
_____
_____
_____
_____

Reflect on

Psalm 78:3-4, 6-7 (TPT):

We've heard true stories from our fathers about our rich heritage. We will continue to tell our children and not hide from the rising generation the great marvels of our God—his miracles and power that have brought us all this far. The story of Israel is a lesson in God's ways. . . .

God's ways will be passed down from one generation to the next, even to those not yet born. In this way, every generation will set its hope in God and not forget his wonderful works but keep his commandments.

Consider the scripture above and answer the following questions:

How is the story of your life a lesson in God's ways?

_____

_____

_____

_____

_____

Which parts of His faithfulness would you like to pass down to enrich the living faith of generations to come?

_____

_____

_____

_____

_____

Compare and contrast the legacy you were given and the legacy you'd like to leave.

_____
_____
_____
_____
_____
_____

Why do we (or many of us, at least) avoid tests of character and patience? What do we miss when we avoid them? What is the payoff for facing them?

_____
_____
_____
_____
_____
_____
_____
_____
_____

Imagine what you'd like people to say at your funeral and write out the key statements.

_____
_____
_____
_____
_____
_____

How can you adjust your schedule to spend quality time with your spouse and children daily, weekly, and yearly? Focus on daily and weekly.

What changes will make the most difference?

Do you expect your own internal resistance or pushback from the people in your family? If you do, how will you handle it?

_____
_____
_____
_____
_____
_____
_____

What is the most important takeaway you've gotten from reading this book and reflecting on its principles?

_____
_____
_____
_____
_____
_____
_____
_____
_____
_____
_____
_____

www.ingramcontent.com/pod-product-compliance
Lightning Source LLC
Chambersburg PA
CBHW062122080426
42734CB00012B/2959